contents

introduction

You have set the date. Now there are a thousand and one things to think about and decide: from the catering to the limousine, from the bouquets to the choice of bridesmaids. With so much to plan it's easy to forget or neglect the two people who are at the center of it all: you and the one you love. These days before the wedding can be a special time in which to discover more about each other and lay the foundations for the years ahead.

You have asked to be married in the Catholic Church. The Church wants your wedding to be perfect for both of you. And so the Church will encourage you to concentrate on what is at the heart of any successful marriage – true love for one another.

touched by love

An old Eastern proverb says, "One look is worth a dozen words and one touch is worth a dozen looks." It is true. Even the lightest touch can speak volumes. It can lift us into another world – the world of love. Your desire to marry is a sign that you and your partner have been "touched" by one another and have opened your hearts to each other.

Some people may say, "I don't understand what you see in each other." But love makes it possible for you to see what no one else sees: your partner really is the most precious person in the world. Naturally you want to tell the world of your love. And you want your love to continue forever.

You will announce all these things on your wedding day. At the most important moment of the wedding ceremony you will join hands and exchange rings as a sign that your love is for life. From that day forward, as you touch one another in love-making, you will recreate your own lives and create a new family.

Growing in Love

Your wedding day completes one period of your relationship and begins another. The pictures taken on that day may fade but your love should grow stronger.

There is no single secret to growing in love. Every marriage is unique. Look at your hands, the hands which gave one of the first signs of "touch" to each other, and see how each finger bears its own print – unrepeated on anyone else, ever, at any time.

It's been said that, like fingerprints, all marriages are different. Your marriage is special. There will be no other marriage on earth quite like yours. It doesn't matter what kind of marriage your family expect you to have; it doesn't matter what kind of marriage society says is "usual;" all that matters is that your marriage is right for each of you. The way you make love is what will make it your marriage and no one else's.

Sex and Love

When we talk about "making love" we usually mean sexual intercourse between two people. But if we stop to think about it "making love" is much more than that. Sexual intercourse can become just a selfish ego trip or simply a desire to follow the crowd. But sexual intercourse is transformed when, in marriage, it becomes a sign of your love. This is a love which shows itself in unselfishness and which, after a disagreement or a fight, can share forgiveness. This love, which you express in sexual intercourse, is creative in two ways:

- **You recreate each other**

Perhaps for the first time each of you feels really free to share yourself honestly and openly. You may bring to your marriage many scars from earlier relationships or from your childhood. Love in marriage helps to heal these hurts. It offers the chance to start again. In the safety of one another's arms, you will discover new depths and fresh values. Such experiences can transform you both and help your love to last.

- **You create a new family**

As soon as you are married, you create a new family unit, and your love-making opens the possibility of creating a completely new human being. The future of your baby will depend very much on the quality of your love throughout your future life together.

God and Love

Susie, aged four, was told the story of Cinderella by her father. She loved the story so much that she wanted it every night. After a while her father read the story into a tape recorder. From now on when she wanted the story she had only to press the button.

This worked for a couple of nights but then Susie complained. She took the storybook to her father for a proper story. "It's on the tape," he said, "all you have to do is press the button." "I know," said Susie, "but I can't sit on its lap!"

It's so much easier to believe in someone's love when you feel their arms around you. The touch of your partner reassures you of his or her love. It should also reassure you of God's love. For Christians believe that God reaches out and touches us through the love of others. We believe that Jesus Christ is at the heart of all love.

Falling in love is a very human experience. But when we decide to consecrate that love in Christian marriage our human love becomes a sign in the world of God's love. Our experience tells us that there is something "extra" here – something beyond human explanation. When you pledge yourselves to unconditional love for life you show what Christ's own self-sacrificing love is like. Yours is a love with no limits.

The Future and Love

As you hold hands during your wedding ceremony and declare your love for each other it is as though a current passes from one to the other; it is as though the power and the love of God passes between you, uniting you in that same love. And indeed, God does offer you his own supreme love to strengthen and sustain you and to make perfect love possible.

To describe this mystery and miracle of love the Church uses the word sacrament. This word simply means that in marriage the intimate love between husband and wife is a unique sharing in God's love. In marriage, when you reach out to touch your husband or wife in love, you lift one another into another world: into the arms of the loving God with whom you will both be safe for ever.

your choice

What made you choose a church wedding?

- I am a baptized Catholic
- My partner is keen on a church wedding
- We know the priest and we'd like him to marry us
- We really believe in Christian marriage
- We go to church regularly
- It's more romantic to be married in church
- The church is near to our reception venue
- Our families are associated with the parish

Try to work out your own answer to the question. Maybe there isn't a single answer. Perhaps your decision is based on lots of reasons. By thinking about this question you'll be able to see the different influences there are working on you.

Planning a Wedding can be Complicated

When you fell in love and decided you wanted to spend the rest of your lives together it was an intensely personal moment. But as soon as you announced your plans you seemed surrounded by people telling you what you should do, what the custom is, or whatever your families expect of you. Everyone has some advice to offer. Suddenly, your private love seems to become public property and you can be swept along by other people's ideas and expectations.

This can be an unnerving experience. Trying to fit in with others' ideas becomes a feature of many marriages. It's a bad beginning for a couple to become so weighed down by pressures and influences from others that they lose touch with their own personal relationship.

The choice of where to get married should reflect your own expectations about your marriage. You probably chose to be married in a Catholic church for a combination of the reasons suggested. But it is important that they are your reasons and not the result of outside pressures. And your reasons for marrying in a Catholic church must, in some measure, match the hopes and ideas of the Church herself about marriage.

By wanting to be married in church you show that there is a "sacredness" about your love. It is more than a matter of fulfilling the legal requirements of the state. Your relationship has something extra: it has a joy and a hopefulness which "lift" it out of the realm of ordinary experience.

The first Christmas we were married we spent with my parents. This meant that the following year we were expected to go to Tony's family. That was fine, we didn't mind. In the following spring our little girl was born and my mother was thrilled to have us all, complete with baby, for the next holiday. And so it went on for another couple of years, taking turns between families, anxious not to cause offense.

By this time we had moved further away from both families and the traveling over the winter holiday period had become more and more of a drag. Suddenly, one autumn, Tony said, "Why don't we spend Christmas at home this year?" I don't know why we hadn't done it before. I suppose we had just got into the habit of the big get-together every year, even though we had begun to dread the whole business of driving back and forth.

The difficulty was telling his family and then mine that we would be breaking the tradition. There were tears and misunderstandings and my mother thought we were giving her the cold shoulder! How I wished we had never got into the trap of that regular commitment which is so hard to break without hurting people's feelings.

What customs will you establish in your brand new family life as a married couple? How will you make sure each family feels that they still matter, without allowing them to take over your married life? How will you avoid getting your families caught up in your personal disagreements within your marriage?

starting points for preparation

- Do you both want a church wedding or is one of you going along with the other's wishes?
- Are you being pressured by either of your families about how your wedding day and marriage should be?
- Do you want children? How many?
- What are the things you like best about your partner?
- What are the things you don't like about your partner? Can you live with them?
- Do you get along with each other's family?
- What do you understand by a "life-long" commitment?
- How will you share your money when you are married?
- How do you think your sex life will develop when you're married?
- How will it be if one of you is ill or when you grow older?
- What do you think is special about a Christian marriage?
- Are you confident enough in each other to talk about all these questions together?

what next?

By now you may be surprised to discover how much is involved in preparing for marriage. The Church is very serious about this preparation. In many places at least six months' notice is needed before you can get married in church.

This isn't just preparation for the wedding day itself. Now is the time that you lay the foundations for your whole married life.

Your priest will explain the form of marriage preparation in your own parish. In practice this may mean that he will arrange for several sessions in which he or others will help you plan your wedding and think about your future happiness.

In many parishes special courses are run for engaged couples. These are organized by married people who are willing to help you work through some of the problem areas.

Some couples are put off by the idea of marriage preparation. A few even think that the Church is interfering. In fact, quite the opposite is true. The aim is to help you plan your own marriage and grow closer as a couple. It would be most unfair if the Church encouraged people to marry without any preparation and then expected them to live up to a standard to which they didn't realize they were committing themselves.

It's important to be sure that both of you are entering marriage freely. Sometimes people decide to marry solely because a baby is on the way; or they want to get away from home; or they may be frightened of being "left on the shelf."

When you're in love it's easy to gloss over future problems. By following marriage preparation carefully you can be helped to face difficult questions. You can work out before you're married how you're going to cope. This can stop problems becoming more serious later.

Many Catholics marry someone who doesn't share the same faith and religious practice. It's helpful for such couples to spend time sharing and exploring their ideas so that each may grow in mutual respect for the other.

what if your partner is not a Catholic?

When you arrange your wedding the priest will explain what happens when you marry someone who isn't a Catholic. You will need permission from the Church to marry. You will have to promise two things. First that you will keep your faith alive. Second that you will do everything you can to have all your children baptized and brought up as Catholics. This means that you will agree to pass on the precious gift of your own faith to your children.

The priest will ask you to think about these promises and what they will mean for both of you. Your partner needs to know that you have made these promises but will not have to make this same promise.

Many Catholics are married to partners who do not share their faith and their marriages are often great examples of understanding, love, and cooperation. Make every effort to share your faith and what it means to you, without putting any pressure on your partner to become more involved than he or she may wish.

what if you are not a Catholic?

You and all your family will be warmly welcomed in the church on your wedding day. Meanwhile, here are some points to think about:

1 Remember that the Catholic Church respects you and your beliefs at all times.

2 A wedding is a time of great sharing. Now is the time to talk over your ideas about life with your partner. Exchange your opinions honestly. Tell each other what you believe and what you don't.

3 Discuss together what kind of married life you hope for. What do you think about having children: when and how many? Catholics believe that marriage is for life; what do you think?

4 Resist the temptation to put off discussing sensitive issues where your opinions differ. If you are honest with each other now you can avoid misunderstandings later.

5 Don't feel you are responsible for your Catholic partner's faith. Although your partner will welcome your support, the practice of the Catholic life is entirely up to him or her.

6 The Catholic Church welcomes you as the husband or wife of one of its family. Feel free to join in the life of the Church as much or as little as you wish.

7 Talk to the priest about any difficulties or anxieties you may have about marrying a Catholic. He will understand and be happy to explain any points before or after your wedding.

Remember that the Catholic Church respects you and your beliefs at all times.

I knew Debbie was slightly reserved. It was something that had attracted me to her in the first place. I have always been quite a demonstrative person; in our family we always hugged each other, exchanged a kiss at special moments, and generally felt at ease expressing our emotions. Debbie's family are very thoughtful, loving people, but much less demonstrative than mine. I never gave either point much thought at the time.

After our marriage, her reserve began to feel like coldness and rejection. We began to drift apart in all sorts of little ways. Things came to a head one evening when a fight erupted at bedtime; out poured all our suppressed anger and frustration. I think it was an eye-opener for both of us. I had thought that Debbie didn't want me and she was thinking that I was beginning to regret getting married! That fight was a blessing because it made us both look deeply at what was happening to us and why.

Do the members of your family show their feelings easily? Are there differences in this between you and your partner? If so, how will you work things out?

choosing your lifestyle

You are looking forward to one of the most memorable moments of your lives – your wedding day. And although you may be feeling anxious about the arrangements you are sharing it all with the person you love. Together, you are planning your own special day. And, providing you have planned carefully and not overlooked anything important, your wedding will be full of joy. In the years ahead your marriage will also depend on the way you plan it.

To talk of "planning" your marriage can seem cold and calculating. Your love for each other seems so great that nothing could spoil it. But when something seems ideal for us we are tempted to overlook any possible obstacles. Advertisers exploit this tendency but experience tells us that it's a good idea to check out whether the car or the washing machine is going to be what we really want regardless of our initial attraction to that particular model. If we go to such lengths when buying goods for the home it makes sense to make at least as serious an assessment of yourself and your partner as a married couple.

Be Realistic

At present you are both on your "best behavior." Each of you is trying to please the other. You may be trying to hide any minor faults you have such as being untidy or a poor timekeeper; you may even be hiding more serious defects. Equally, you are probably making allowances for each other in your desire to be understanding, tolerant, and loving.

Such efforts have their value, but not as a foundation for marriage, because they are masking reality. It will be impossible to keep that best behavior going for the rest of your lives together. Sooner or later you will have to face the truth. Try to have the courage to be yourselves by sharing the good points and the bad. Ask yourselves what you most enjoy about your relationship, and ask one another what is your greatest fear for the future. If there is something that is likely to drive your partner mad it is better to sort it out before the wedding.

Each of you will have an idea of the part which a husband or wife should play in marriage, usually based on your own family background. Discuss things like the sharing of chores, the question of evenings out from one another and the management of money. Who will pay for what, how will you manage if there is only one wage-earner, what about "spending money" for each of you?

Many couples say, "we'll share everything." This is an easy trap to fall into. It really doesn't solve the problem of who does what. You may both have very different ideas on what "sharing" means! Does "sharing" mean that you'll take turns doing the ironing or cleaning the windows? Will you share the rent or mortgage? Make a list of all the things which have to be done. Talk about who's going to do what and how the workload can be shared.

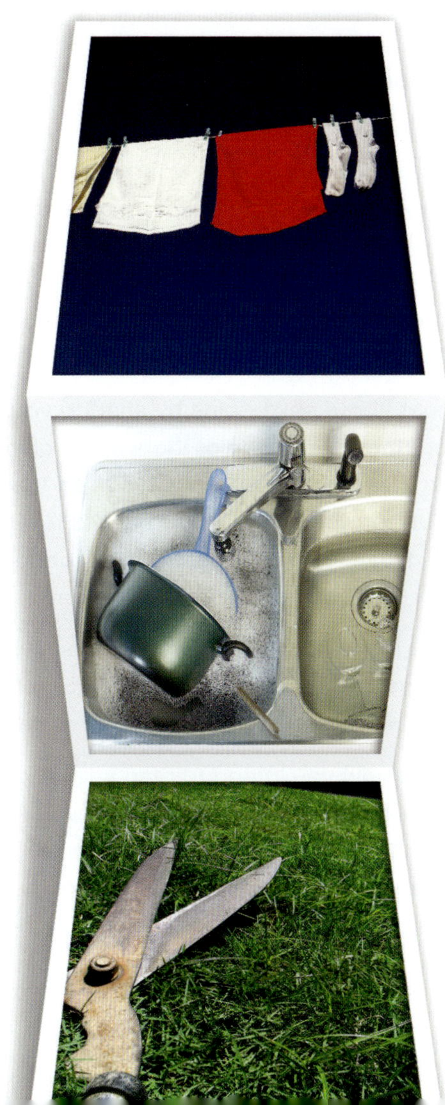

choosing your lifestyle

Sex

One of the most important parts of facing up to the truth about yourselves and your relationship is being honest about sex. Sex is the way in which you show your deepest feelings. Any lack of honesty here can grow like a crack in the foundations of your lives.

Both of you have an image of what is "normal" in a couple's sex life. You may already know some things which you both enjoy and you will discover many more over the years. Equally, you may find some of your partner's ideas less attractive. Now is the time to make it a rule for life to be honest about what excites you and what leaves you cold. Such differences can be overcome by honestly telling your partner how you feel. If either partner ignores these differences it is a sign that sex has become divorced from love.

Some couples develop a pattern in which one person makes all the decisions about sex, saying when, where, and how intercourse takes place. This can mean that two people appear to ignore each other all day and then one decides it's time for sex with little or no concern for the other's feelings.

Just as you'll have to learn to change the way you live when you marry so, too, you have much to learn about sex. Together you will begin to set up a pattern which brings you both fulfillment. You will need to search for a real understanding of each other's needs. A full and satisfying sex life will do much to make your marriage a rich and sustaining relationship.

Being honest about sex begins by sharing your feelings together every step of the way. Explore each other's body and the way in which your partner is aroused. Tell your partner how you would like to be touched and kissed. Talk about how you can show your love for each other throughout the day.

Discover the ways apart from intercourse in which you can make love to each other. And don't forget to laugh about your sex life – it can be very funny at times.

Talking about how you intend to plan a family is a must before the wedding. How many children would you like to have? Do you see children as completing and perfecting your own relationship? Have you considered the implications of not being able to conceive or give birth to children?

Marriage is a lifelong process of making love. In the early days some disappointment and sexual frustration are likely. Don't let that lead to a breakdown in discussion or sharing of feelings: use such moments as a chance to learn more about each other. In this way sexual intercourse will be a true sign of peace between you and deepen your love for one another.

Faith

It is important to keep in touch with one another. And it is equally important to keep in touch with God, who is the source of love. God's love transforms your love for each other and strengthens you to live out your marriage vows even in times of extreme stress and disappointment. Your wedding in church is a public sign that you appreciate this.

If you are not of the same religion you will each bring to your marriage different ideas and attitudes about religion. But even if you are both Catholics you will probably discover that you have a surprising number of different points of view. Whatever your situation, getting married is a time to reflect on your relationship with God and how you can deepen it.

The practice of your faith can be a sensitive area in family life. If you discuss your ideas now and try to understand each other's view you will help to avoid difficulties in the future. This will become even more important when your first baby comes along. What belief in God are you going to pass on to your children? How are you going to teach your children to pray?

It may well be that neither of you prays very much at present. This need not put you off the idea of praying together as a married couple, as a family. There are many different ways in which you can pray. To acknowledge that you are part of something much greater than just two people is in itself a prayer. Many couples find strength in reading a passage from the Bible together and then talking about it. This is God's word and it gives us guidance for life. You might be happier just to share one or two familiar prayers together. Perhaps you can pray best quietly at night by just holding each other and thanking God for all his gifts.

Some Christians are happy to share their prayer together by speaking out loud to God in their own words. Others find that they're too self-conscious

for this. It's good to share your prayer in this way but you're not a failure if you can't! The important thing is to respect each other's beliefs.

Worshipping together is important too. If your partner belongs to a different church then don't be afraid to go to both churches. In this way you show respect for each other's faith.

Thanking God for each other doesn't stop with prayer. There are many family events which can be marked with a celebration. A birthday or anniversary can be celebrated by going to church together and then on for a special meal. Lent is a time when Christians have a good look at their lives. Why not find something special which you can do together for Lent?

Finally, remember that your faith is a precious gift. Don't keep it to yourself. Share it with your partner. Faith will make both your lives all the richer.

Talk About It!

At the heart of your marriage will be the way in which you communicate. Make sure you have time to be with each other – to talk to one another. It's not enough to go out with friends or watch TV at home together. By planning to make time to talk, even when you are both tired, you lift your marriage out of the rut of routine.

It would be silly to think that you're never going to disagree about things. If something is important to you then you should be able to talk it through together. It would be a most unusual marriage if you never had an argument. But don't forget that it takes two to make up after a fight. Try to have every quarrel resolved by the end of the day. It's not always easy to admit that you're wrong but if both of you are always willing to forgive it'll be much easier to say, "I'm sorry."

Some people enter marriage hoping to change their husband or wife. This is a recipe for disaster and it's essential to give your partner space to be himself or herself and time to be alone. You are attracted to each other because of the "specialness" you see in your partner. Keep it that way. Develop the ability to exchange points of view without trying to make a takeover bid for each other's personality.

There is more to communication than talking. A smile or a frown can speak volumes. This can be so easily forgotten once you are married. Holding hands, a brief hug and the kiss before leaving for work or on return, are all ways in which we keep saying, "I love you." They are unspoken reminders of the promise made on your wedding day: to have and to hold from this day forward. It is through such touches that your marriage lasts for life and your love for ever.

Q&A

what you always wanted to know but didn

My uncle is a Methodist minister. Would he be allowed to take part in our wedding service in a Catholic Church?

Yes, he is welcome to share in the liturgy with the priest. He may read the prayers, give a short address or be responsible for one of the readings. Discuss the matter with your priest and your uncle and decide how you would like the ceremony planned.

My fiancé is a Muslim and a different nationality from me. He has agreed to marry in the Catholic Church. Are there any special formalities I need to explain to him?

You will need to explain what a Christian marriage involves, its obligations and legal standing in this country. You will also need to obtain a dispensation from the bishop in order to marry a non-Christian. Your priest will explain the procedure for this.

In addition, ask your fiancé to explain his ideas about marriage and family life. You will know that his customs and religious laws are very different from yours, and it is important that you understand the differences before you marry. It is a big step to build a bridge between two religions and two very different cultures.

Before we were married Jim always went to football every Sunday and then out for drinks with his friends afterwards. We usually met up later in the evening. I didn't mind because we had always done that. I suppose I thought that after we were married he wouldn't go out quite so often and he would come home sooner. We didn't really discuss it, I just took it for granted that he would spend more time at home with me at the weekends.

The first winter after we were married was so depressing. Jim just carried on in his usual way and I began to feel more and more left out of his social life. I began going to my mother's on Sundays, and she soon realized that I was fed up. I poured out my feelings to my family one day and that turned them a bit against Jim. I hinted to Jim that I was unhappy at not seeing much of him but he didn't seem to notice it until things got really bad and we were arguing every week. Then we finally began to sort it out.

Jim admits that Sue's fury came like a bolt from the blue to him. "She never complained to me so I thought she didn't mind. After all I had always gone out a lot even when she first met me. It wasn't until her family started giving me the cold shoulder and she got really upset that I realized that things had got to quite a serious point of friction."

How do you spend your spare time at present? What changes do you think will need to be made when you marry?

Is it the custom to invite the priest to the wedding reception?

It is entirely up to you whether you invite him to your reception. Couples often do invite the priest to join the celebrations but he is not always free to accept their invitation. He may have other appointments or another wedding later in the day.

I am a practicing Catholic. My fiancé and I want to start a family in a couple of years but disagree with the Church's teaching which disapproves of the contraceptive pill. Can I be married in church?

Wanting a couple of years of married life before having your first child is quite understandable. You and your husband will have to make many personal changes after you marry. You'll need time to get to know each other really well and to settle into married life together.

The Church wholeheartedly supports responsible parenthood. Planning when to have your family is an important part of married life. The question is, how do you do the planning? If you are going to marry in the Church you must explore what the Church means by "responsible parenthood" and how this is to be achieved.

The Church's fundamental teaching is that sexual intercourse is to give life to the married couple and is to be open to giving life to another human being. These two functions of sexual intercourse cannot be separated.

The Church, then, encourages family planning which uses natural methods (see question on page 17) and excludes any method which places a barrier between the natural intimacy of the couple. Condoms and diaphragms put a barrier between sperm and egg so that fertilization cannot take place. The pill takes over the body's job of releasing hormones to make sure that an egg is not allowed to travel into a position to be fertilized.

No Catholic can disregard the Law of God as taught by the Church. If a couple decide that they will not have children under any circumstances and at any time because they don't want the bother and expense, they would not be entering a Christian marriage. Such a couple could not be married in the Catholic Church.

If, on the other hand, a couple feel unable to live up to the teaching of the Church in their particular circumstances at the present time, this would not prevent their marrying in the Church. We all fail to live up to the teaching of Christ and his Church in many other respects, but we should constantly strive to do so.

What is most important when couples are planning their family is that they do so in good conscience before God. This does not mean just pleasing themselves. It means rather that in applying the teaching of the Church to their particular circumstances their actions are pleasing to God. For children are a gift from God; and only God is the judge of consciences.

I have been living with my girlfriend for the past two years. Surely this is the best way to get to know each other. Do we still need marriage preparation?

Many people think that living together or a "trial marriage" is the best form of marriage preparation. It is only by living with someone, they say, that you can really get to know them properly.

Certainly couples who live and sleep together get to know a lot about each other. But it is very different from marriage in one big way. A trial marriage is temporary. If things go wrong the couple will split up. Christian marriage is permanent. When things go wrong the couple will stick together and work things out.

For Christians, married love is like Christ's love. It is faithful and unselfish...and permanent. An arrangement in which a couple agrees to live together and to separate if things go wrong inevitably devalues true love. Living together, then, can damage a couple. Such an arrangement appears to lend freedom to a relationship but it also breeds insecurity and lack of confidence. What happens in sickness or unemployment? These are the reasons for Christ's clear teaching that life together in a sexual union belongs only to marriage.

The fact that marriage is for life makes all the difference. This will change your thinking on many things. This is why you need marriage preparation. It will give you the chance to think about exactly how your lives will change when you are actually married and not just living together.

I am pregnant and my boyfriend and I want to get married. Can we still have a church wedding?

The fact that you're pregnant doesn't mean that you can't have a church wedding. Even if the baby is born before the wedding, you can still marry in church.

However, because of the new situation you need to ensure that you really are entering marriage freely. You may feel an internal pressure that you now have no alternative other than to get married. You may feel pressure from your boyfriend or parents to get married. If, in any way, you feel forced into marriage then it's not a real marriage at all. You must make a free decision. This decision will affect not only your lives but your baby's too.

Take time to think this through and talk it through and consider all the possible alternatives. Then try to make your decision about your marriage as though you weren't pregnant. It will be far better to postpone or cancel your wedding than enter into an unhappy marriage, which ultimately would damage all of you.

What is natural family planning? Is it reliable for all couples?

Present-day methods of natural family planning predict very accurately the fertile period in a woman's cycle by monitoring changes in her body. Once a couple have been taught this method they may plan or delay pregnancy according to their situation. Women who have irregular cycles or who are breastfeeding can also use this method with confidence.

The advantage of natural family planning is that it is very accurate, it is free and there are no health risks for either partner.

My parents are divorced and have remarried. I would like my stepfather to give me away as he has been like a father to me since I was four years old. Would this be allowed?

Traditionally, it is the bride's father who gives her away. But if you have little or no contact with your father and prefer your stepfather to give you away there could be no objection. It is a question for you and your family to decide.

I was brought up as a Catholic but I haven't been going to church regularly for some years. I go to Mass sometimes, usually when I visit my parents at Christmas or Easter. My fiancé doesn't belong to any Church and has no religious beliefs. We've decided that we want a church wedding. Will we be allowed to marry in the Catholic Church?

The Church's main concern is that your wedding marks a sincere commitment to Christian marriage. If you are sincere in your wishes, you will be able to marry in the Catholic Church. However, you may find it helpful to explore why you want a church wedding. Is it because it "feels" better? Maybe you think it will please your parents? Maybe it's because it seems more romantic? If it is more than just "feeling right" try to explore what your reasons really are. This is a big step for both of you. It's an opportunity to start a new life. So ask yourselves what you honestly believe.

Many people go through a period in their lives when they fall away from faith. Often we need to discover a life of faith for ourselves as adults before we can accept the full meaning of being a practicing Christian. Sometimes, we may simply have grown careless about our faith and let it slip for no other reason than laziness or the distractions of other activities. Give some serious thought to your ideas and beliefs. Be honest with your priest about your doubts and difficulties and discuss them with your fiancé before making any final decisions.

Your wedding could be an opportunity for you to make a fresh start with your faith if that is what you would like to do.

My fiancée has been married before. Her first marriage ended in divorce. She has since obtained a decree of nullity so we are free to marry in the Catholic Church. Are there any special rules for second weddings?

You say that your fiancée has obtained a decree of nullity. This means that a valid marriage never existed in the first place and so in effect her marriage to you will be her first marriage. When you go to the priest you will need to take along the papers proving both the civil divorce and the nullity. As with all church weddings, the priest will advise you on how to approach your ceremony.

We would like to marry in the church near my parents' home. Will that be possible?

The usual arrangement is that a marriage takes place in the parish where at least one of you lives. If you want to marry somewhere else you will need a letter from your parish priest giving his permission. Ask your parents' parish priest well in advance if he is able to marry you. Make sure you check at the marriage license office about the legal and residency requirements.

This is a big step for both of you.
It's an opportunity to start a new life.
So ask yourselves what you honestly believe.

what you always wanted to know but didn

My mother says that Catholics have to go to confession before they can get married in church. Is she right?

Marriage is always a time for a fresh start, so that may explain why your mother and many others think it is necessary to go to confession beforehand, but, no, she is not right. The Sacrament of Reconciliation has to do with the forgiveness of sin and it is for each individual to know and decide when it is appropriate to celebrate it. The Church requires that we celebrate this sacrament only when we are conscious that our relationship with God and the Church has grieviously been impaired through serious sin. However, the Church also encourages us to use this sacrament to help us grow in God's love and it may well be that prior to celebrating your marriage you would wish to confess your sins.

Getting married is the start of a whole new relationship. It's not just you and your husband who are starting afresh. You are starting a fresh phase in your life and in your relationship with God. This sacrament could help you reflect on and celebrate all this. Should you wish to go to confession, go and see a priest. Tell him that you're going to get married, and even if it's a long time since you last confessed your sins he'll understand and help you.

I am a single Catholic going out with a divorced man. We are very much in love and would like to get married. Could we get married in church?

As you present your case, you probably will not be able to marry in a Catholic church because the Church respects the marriages of those from other Christian traditions as well as those of other faiths and none. In other words, while the Church has clear guidelines as to how Catholics should enter marriage, it also presumes that other marriages, including those entered at City Hall, are true and valid unless it can be proved otherwise. Of course, if it could be established that the marriage of this man had not been a true marriage then you could marry in a Catholic church. Just as Catholics can ask the Church's tribunals to investigate their failed marriages to see whether there are grounds to declare them null and void, so the same tribunals can investigate the failed marriages of those who wish to marry Catholics. If you would like to know more about this you would need to consult your priest or contact the Diocesan Tribunal directly.

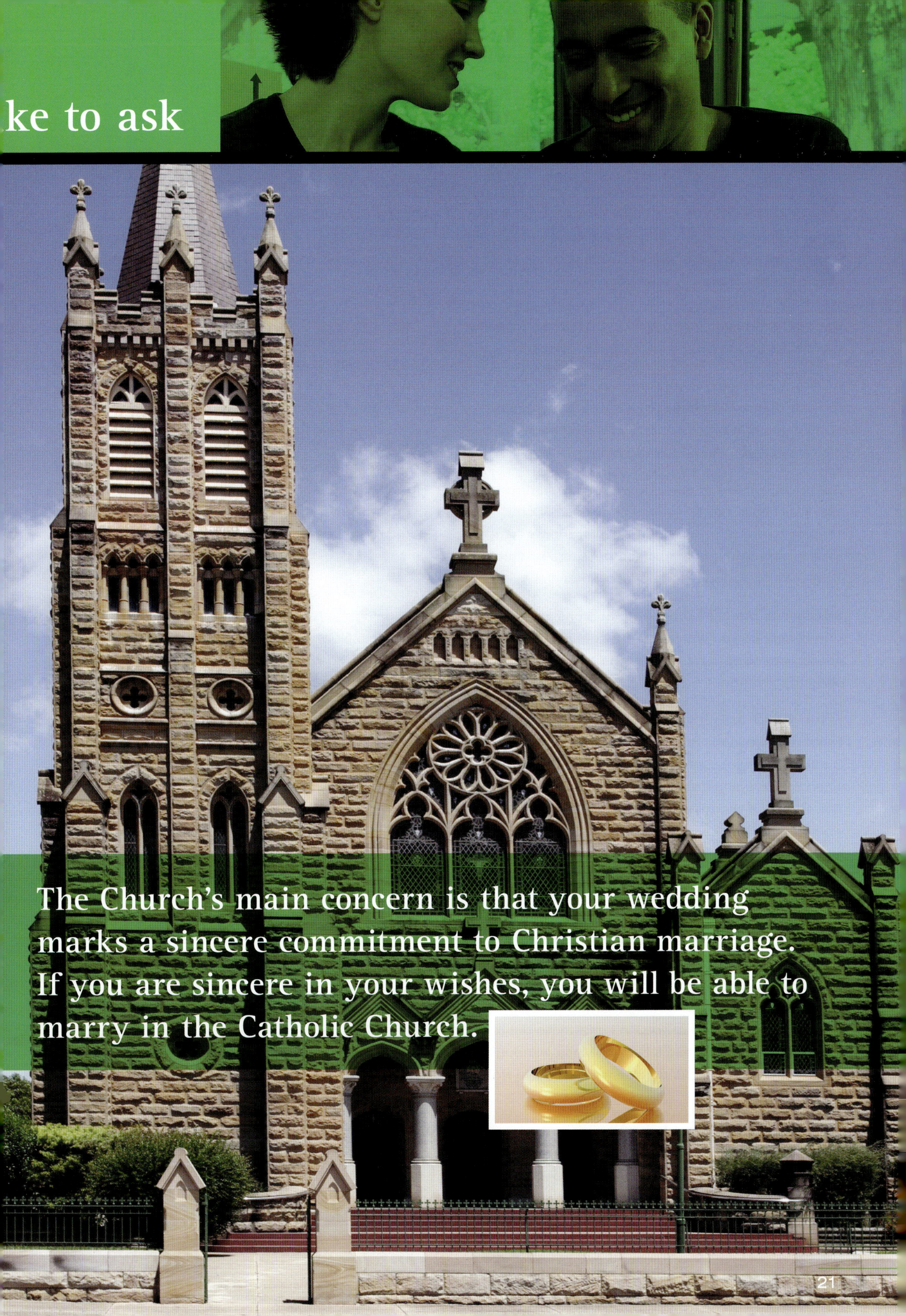

The Church's main concern is that your wedding marks a sincere commitment to Christian marriage. If you are sincere in your wishes, you will be able to marry in the Catholic Church.

planning your wedding

Most people are nervous on their wedding day, but the better prepared you are, the less nervous you are likely to be. Here are a few practical points you will do well to consider when planning your wedding.

The law lays down strict rules which must be followed in order for you to be married. Check these out.

Work out a budget for your wedding based on what you can afford. Expenses have a way of increasing without you realizing it and it's as well to begin marriage as you intend to carry on.

The priest is there to help you through this important day. If you have any questions or anxieties don't hesitate to ask him. Arrangements for the wedding service vary from place to place but there's nearly always an opportunity for a brief rehearsal.

You have to make a number of decisions about the kind of service you want. The priest will explain the possibilities to you. Here are some of the things you'll need to think about.

What Kind of Service?

There are two kinds of service in the Catholic Church. One is a Wedding Service with Nuptial Mass. This is when the wedding itself takes place as part of a Mass. The other is a Wedding Service without Mass. The part where you make your promises is the same in each and both are joyful celebrations. You may find it helpful to discuss the alternatives with your priest before making a final decision.

Wedding Service with Nuptial Mass

The Mass is important to Catholics as it unites us with Jesus Christ and one another in a special way. Normally two Catholics getting married would choose a Nuptial Mass. If one of you isn't a Catholic but is baptized you can choose a Nuptial Mass, although usually only the Catholic partner would receive Holy Communion.

Wedding Service without Mass

It is quite normal to get married in the Catholic Church without celebrating a Nuptial Mass. This does not make it less of a true marriage and the service without Mass is equally impressive and joyful. If one of you is not a Catholic you and your family may feel more at home with this ceremony. This is the form your marriage service will take if one of you isn't baptized.

Readers

The priest will read the Gospel at your wedding. There will be other readings from the scriptures too. You might like to ask some of your guests to read for you. They will need to practice the piece so that they understand what they're reading.

There are also the prayers of the faithful or petitions. You can write these yourselves with the priest's help. He will have some general prayers that you can choose from or adapt if you want to. Another guest could read these.

Witnesses

You must choose two adults to witness your wedding by signing the register. They don't have to be Catholics. Normally the best man and the maid of honor are chosen for this, but it could be your parents or close friends.

Altar Servers

These aren't always necessary but some of your friends or servers from the parish may be used to serving at Mass and might like to help at your wedding.

Best Man

The best man plays a key role in making sure the day runs smoothly. He looks after the bride's ring and traditionally gives a speech at the reception. He is also on hand to help with other things as necessary, such as paying musicians and calming the groom's nerves.

Maid of Honor

The maid of honor also plays a key role in assisting the bride with her dress, veil, and flowers, and help calm her nerves. She looks after the groom's ring and may also give a speech at the reception.

Music

Music can make a big difference to your wedding. There may be musicians and singers in the parish who are available for weddings, or you may have musical friends who can lend their talents. It is important that you negotiate the music you'd like with the priest and/or director of music (if there is one) in the early stages of planning. Traditionally wedding music is led by an organist but many other instruments and styles of music can also be appropriate.

Ushers

It's a good idea to ask family or friends to make your guests welcome. Those who are familiar with the church can show people to their place and give out books. It is traditional for the bride's guests to sit on the left-hand side of the church and for the groom's to sit on the right.

Flowers

It is advisable to check on local custom and ensure that clear arrangements are agreed for florists or flower arrangers to come to the church. It is worth finding out if any other couples are to be married on the same day: you may be able to make joint arrangements and share the costs.

Photography

Discuss the taking of photographs and video recordings with the priest beforehand. Most churches allow photographs and videos to be taken during the wedding service but it is important that the cameras do not interfere with the ceremony or distract either yourselves or the congregation. If there is any suggestion that extra lighting is necessary, obviously this should be checked with the priest.

We're both Catholics. Paul is much more involved than me though. He was active in his parish when we met and now he attends a local prayer group. I went to Mass but that was about it.

After we'd been married a few months Paul came home one day really excited. He'd been reading a religious book. It was all about married couples praying together. All the people at the prayer group had been talking about it. He wanted us to give it a try. I wasn't keen. My mind was full of memories of being made to join in with prayers at school and at home. The last thing I wanted was to be forced to join in again.

Paul didn't give up, so in the end I said I'd give it a try. It was awful. I felt so uncomfortable. I just couldn't relax. In the end I made up excuses every time he suggested it. After a while we had a fight. Paul said that I was half-hearted about the spiritual side of our marriage. He went on about so many couples being much more "together" than us.

Paul finally realized that his well-meaning pressure on Jan was causing a serious split in their relationship. "I wasn't seeing things straight. Jan and I were really happily married. I was getting carried away by the people at the prayer group. I'd been so wrapped up in what I thought 'real' Christians did that I'd been ignoring Jan's feelings. Now I realize that I was stupid to try to force Jan into seeing things my way."

Have you talked about praying together at home? How are you going to keep your faith alive as a family? How will you pass your faith on to your children? Are you respecting each other's point of view in this matter?

your wedding day

Your wedding day will be filled with ceremony. From the dressing of the bride to your departure for the honeymoon there are many customs which vary from country to country. But the heart of the celebrations is always the same: the marriage vows which are proclaimed publicly before God and the people present.

In the Catholic Church you will be encouraged to make your wedding both as personal and communal an occasion as possible. You are the center of what is happening, and the priest or deacon and your family and friends are present as witnesses for the Church and society. But it is your words and your presence which make the occasion so solemn and sacred. It is not the Church's minister who is marrying you; you are marrying each other.

The wedding ceremony may be divided into three parts; and in each part the spotlight is turned in a new direction. It begins by focusing our attention on God, then on yourselves and, finally, on the world into which you will enter as a newly married couple.

God

The ceremony begins with a welcome, first of God, and then of one another. The whole congregation is invited to begin the ceremony by making the sign of the cross, a reminder that Jesus loved us enough to die for us.

A prayer is offered for the happiness of the couple to which everyone responds "Amen."

There follows the readings from Scripture, the word of God. These challenge us to reflect on the ideals of married life and Christian living. In his homily (sermon) the minister will help you and the congregation think more about these ideals. We are not able to live up to them by ourselves, but we believe that God is always faithful and does not abandon us. God will be with you in your marriage and will give you strength to live out the promises which you are about to make.

Yourselves

The spotlight then turns on you. You are now the center of attention. Everyone stands and the minister addresses you in these or similar words:

You have come together in this church so that the Lord may seal and strengthen your love in the presence of the Church's minister and this community. Christ abundantly blesses this love. He has already consecrated you in baptism and now he enriches and strengthens you by a special sacrament so that you may assume the duties of marriage in mutual and lasting fidelity. And so, in the presence of the Church, I ask you to state your intentions.

The minister asks you three questions. After each you both answer in turn, "I am." These questions relate to your marriage vows and are the questions which will remain with you for the rest of your lives. It's important for you to discuss together these three questions which you will be answering on your wedding day.

Before allowing you to go through with your marriage the minister has to be sure of three things:

- That you are free to marry according to the laws of the country and the Church. This includes such things as being old enough to enter marriage. If you have been married before you will need to prove that you are indeed free to marry in the Church.
- That you understand what marriage is and what you're doing. Although you can't see what the future holds you are willing to stay together for the rest of your lives.
- That you are capable of entering into marriage. That you are able to make up your mind in such an important matter. That you are not confused or being rushed into making a decision.

Give and Take

Are you ready freely and without reservation to give yourselves to each other in marriage?

This question means:

- You are promising to give your whole lives to each other just as Jesus gave his life for us. Are you willing to put your marriage before work, parents, interests or anything else? Is there anything which you believe is more important than your marriage?
- Take a good hard look at your partner. This is the person that you're going to spend the rest of your life with. Can you accept them just as they are – including their faults? Do you want to change your partner to measure up to your ideal? Does either of you feel overpowered by the strength of the other's personality? Is your marriage going to be a coming together of two people or a takeover of one by the other?

- Marriage is "give and take." It is a partnership, often of two very different people, who are of equal value and are prepared to work together as a team. Are you ready to be part of such a team? Does either of you feel it's always the same person who "gives in"?

Love and Honor

Are you ready to love and honor each other as man and wife for the rest of your lives?

This question means:

- You are promising always to be faithful to your partner alone; just as God has remained faithful and continues to believe in us. To love one another totally, but only for a period of time, doesn't make sense. Is either of you frightened by such love? Does either of you think that if your marriage doesn't run smoothly you'd look for a divorce?
- To honor your partner means to respect him or her. But you must also honor and respect yourself. What are your personal hopes for the marriage?
- Love grows as the years go by. Do both of you feel that your love has grown since you've known each other? Are there any areas where you always seriously disagree?

Sex and Children

Are you ready to accept children lovingly from God and bring them up according to the law of Christ and his Church?

This question means:

- When you "make love" in marriage you become "one flesh." And it is the moment when you can share in God's creative love by recreating and giving life to one another. Do both of you agree on the part that sexual intercourse will play as a sign of your love within your marriage?
- Sexual intercourse is also the moment when you can share in God's creative love by conceiving a child. Have you talked about how many children you would like to have? Have you agreed on the way in which you would bring them up?

The kind of family which you create depends to some extent on your previous experience of family life. Are there things in your family background which you can't share with your partner? Do either of you feel seriously uncomfortable with your future in-laws?

The Vows

Then the minister asks you to join your right hands and declare that you know what you are doing:

Since it is your intention to enter into marriage, declare your consent before God and his Church.

Taking each other's hand you declare your consent before God and his Church. At this point in the ceremony, looking at each other, you promise to share the future together.

First the bridegroom, then the bride, promises to take their partner...

"To be my lawful wife/husband
to have and to hold,
from this day forward,
for better, for worse,
for richer, for poorer,
in sickness and in health,
to love and to cherish,
until death do us part."

This is the solemn moment of marriage. You are now man and wife. You have united yourselves for life before God and all the people present. The minister declares this to the whole congregation:

What God has joined together, let no one put asunder.

All present unite in their recognition of your vows as they say, so be it...

Amen.

Your wedding rings are blessed and you exchange them. They seal the promises which you have made to each other. They are a sign to all that you will be faithful for ever.

The World

The spotlight finally turns to the world into which you will soon be emerging for the first time as husband